Early Wayne County Settlers

NEW YORK

and
Their Rhineland Origins

Lloyd Espencheid

HERITAGE BOOKS
2011

HERITAGE BOOKS
AN IMPRINT OF HERITAGE BOOKS, INC.

Books, CDs, and more—Worldwide

For our listing of thousands of titles see our website
at
www.HeritageBooks.com

Published 2011 by
HERITAGE BOOKS, INC.
Publishing Division
100 Railroad Ave. #104
Westminster, Maryland 21157

Originally published 1998
Pipe Creek Publications

All rights reserved. No part of this book may be reproduced or transmitted in any form or by any means, electronic or mechanical, including photocopying, recording or by any information storage and retrieval system without written permission from the author, except for the inclusion of brief quotations in a review.

International Standard Book Numbers
Paperbound: 978-1-58549-841-3
Clothbound: 978-0-7884-8795-8

INTRODUCTION

The following history of some early German immigrants into Wayne County, New York has been copied verbatim from an article which appeared in the The Lyons Republican and Clyde Times, commencing November 13 and continuing each week until December 25, 1958. In addition to naming the earliest immigrants from Germany into this area, and identifying their origin in the Mother county, it also follows some members of the younger generation on their continous migration into nidwestern America.

Although this work is brief, it lays ground for further research on many of the early Germans who settled along the Erie Canal in the early part of the 19th century. Also most readers will find assistance in referral to the citation of sources in the author's footnotes.

Mary Keysor Meyer
Editor

EARLY WAYNE COUNTY SETTLERS
&
THEIR RHINELAND ORIGINS

Descendants of early German settlers of Wayne County, New York, may welcome an accounting of certain of their forebears in terms of how they came to locate in Wayne and whence they came in Germany.

Western New York State's wilderness was about ripe for the ax of the pioneer at the turn of the 19th century. The lowly savages of The Six Nations had been reduced to impotence and were yielding their lands; the rival claims to the territory on the part of Massachusetts, Connecticut and New York, were being resolved; initial penetration was occurring westward from the Mohawk and northward from the Susquehanna.[1] For another two decades, however, the settlements were to be few and far between, for Europe was embroiled in the wars of the French Revolution and Napoleon, and the United States of America became engaged with Britain in the War of 1812.

The French overrunning of the Rhineland (1792-1815) had stopped the 18th century migration of Germans to North America, which had been largely into Pennsylvania but also into the Hudson and Mohawk valleys of New York.[2]

What happened following the conclusion of peace is what here concerns us: In New York the

Erie Canal was projected, commenced in 1817 and finished in 1825-6, causing a rapid settlement of the western lands. From the Rhineland there arose a renewal of the 18th century migration. The cause of it was basically the same: (1) the tight population situation among the competing nations of western Europe, giving rise to pressures to conform and to wars, especially along Germany's southwest borders parallelling the Rhine, and (2) the opening of vast tracts of virgin land in North America with attendant relative freedom.

In western Europe following the Napoleonic Wars the new generation sought land, liberty, and the pursuit of happiness, ideals which could not be realized in the historically-bound enemy-states of the Continent. By the 1830's, uprisings were occurring in both France and the Rhineland, giving rise to continued governmental restrictions and to fears of renewed war. (It was not until the Revolution of 1848 that northern Germany contributed materially to the emigration.) The threatening conditions were attended by the haunting question of how the rising generation was to make a living, how to gain access to land and jobs.

Meanwhile, shipping to the USA had been improved, especially through the French port of LeHavre, and in America the great interior lands were being made ac-cessible by primitive roads, canals and river steam boats. To the tightly-bound Rhinelanders with their renewed yearning for peace, space and liberty, the one escape was to follow some of their forefathers across the Atlantic, even though it looked like banishment.³ Thus, there commenced anew the flow of Germans to America, a tide that became sizeable in the 1830's, rose further in the 1840's and 1850's, to be interrupted by the Civil War, and then reached flood proportions in the 1870's and 1880's.

The rising tide flowed into the eastern and then also into the Gulf ports, distributing itself largely in the great central basin of the continent including western New York State. By the beginning of the 20th century, the population of the United States was about one-quarter of Germanic origin. Including the larger original Anglo-Saxon element, the new North American Republic was thus assured being primarily of Teutonic derivation.⁴

The Erie Canal Influx

The great new artery inland from the eastern seaboard, the Erie Canal, naturally conveyed its share of this mounting stream of German immigrants. Most of them were going on to the cheaper lands of the middlewest, for by the 1830's land along the canal was well spoken for and relatively expensive. A German intellectual returning eastward along the canal from a trip inland in 1833, has reported: "When I came down from Utica to Schenectady, on my way home, I believe that not two hours passed without our meeting one or more barges laden with Germans - excellent stock for Michigan, whither most proceeded, as they told me in passing."⁵

Yet, a goodly proportion did stop off along the canal seeking homes, those wishing a more settled countryside than the west afforded. Each immigrant seemed to have in mind some goal, as if previously informed, as indeed was the case, by some piece of literature, a forerunner or a land agent. What about those who disembarked at Lyons - how had they learned of Wayne County, what "friend at court" had they?

Wayne County histories give us one clue; that remarkable human inventory of a Township, "Rose Neighborhood Sketches", by Alfred S. Roe, 1893, says of Wayne Centre: "In this district we shall find many Germans, who seemed to have overflowed from Lyons eastward, and to have thus taken the places of the original settlers. To my inquiry as to the reason for this German influx, I was told that many years since, the father of the late Lieutenant Governor Dorsheimer located in Lyons. Naturally others of his race came to a place where he, who had learned English, could interpret for them, and found homes near him." (p. 211)

Further testimony, identifying the father, is that of George W. Knowles reported in "Gripps" Historical Souvenir of Lyons, N.Y. published in 1904: "Twelve years ago Wm. Ashley - now dead - was probably the oldest male resident of Lyons. His recollection was excellent. I have heard him tell how Lyons came to be so strongly settled with Germans. He said he remembered one morning getting up and finding his back yard filled with German immigrants who had during the night arrived on the boat. His home was on William Street near the school house. The immigrants were inquiring for Philip Dorsheimer, who was then running the Landon House.

Dorsheimer was a prominent man in those days. He afterward moved to Buffalo and had a son who became Lieutenant-Governor of this State. Dorsheimer, it appears, according to Wm. Ashley, pointed out to the newcomers the fact that they could not get better farms anywhere in the state than around Lyons; and he induced most of them to buy land hereabouts, upon which they settled and raised families. Many of their sons finally went into business in the village. They came here with money of their own - and were prosperous. They represented the best class of intelligent, thrifty people that came across the water, and their descendants comprise the very best of Wayne County population today." (p.28)

The Genial Inn-Keeper

Philip Dorsheimer was born about ten miles south of Bingenon-Rhine in the village of Woellstein, Hesse-Darmstadt, more recently in Rheinhassen, on April 15th, 1797. The original birth record has been inspected in recent years by Fr. Pabst, retired pastor of Siefersheim. It is found to give his father as William Dorsheimer and mother Anna Maria, widow of Doerscheck. He was born during the French Revolution and his entire young life was spent under foreign occupation.
Upon becoming of draft age no wonder he left

forthwith upon the withdrawal of French troops. This was consequent upon the crossing of the Rhine by Bluecher that led to Napoleon's Waterloo in 1815.[6]

Philip went to Pennsylvania, apparently to the vicinity of Harrisburg where there were namesakes, probably undertaking the calling of his father, that of miller. He married in Pennsylvania Sarah Gorgas, 1821, Aug. 23.[7] Upon the opening of the Erie Canal in 1825-6, Dorsheimer was attracted to Lyons as a flour miller, and a few years thereafter became an inn-keeper. He operated first the Wayne County Hotel (earlier Price's Tavern, later Congress Hall, located on Water Street where is today the Wayne Hotel), and next, as of about 1833, the Lyons Hotel on the northeast corner of William and Montezuma Streets. The latter was known at different times as the Landon Hotel, Patton House and Graham House.[8]

It was as a Lyons hotel proprietor, in the period of about 1830 to 1836, that Dorshheimer became a lodestone to his fellow-countrymen, leading them to settle in Wayne. The balconies of his Lyons Hotel were a favorite site for observing the arrival of canal boats, and the hotel itself was popular for arriving passengers. Of the arrival of German immigrants in Lyons, an old-time Yankee, Mrs. DeWitt Parshall, has recalled: "The arrival of a boat load of immigrants was an attraction which brought out many sightseers. What interested us, of course, was the dress which the women wore, conspicuous for its bright colored woolen skirt and oddly shaped little cap. Often the immigrants would get off at the dock or lock and start fires and do their cooking."

By a biographer who knew him, Dorsheimer is described as of normal build with relatively large head and pleasing countenance. Gifted with intellect, he had early applied himself to the learning of English, read extensively the press and took a lively interest in the affairs of his adopted country: "Of calm temperament, kind and benevolent he was always ready to assist his fellow countrymen..."[9]

His initial residence among the Pennsylvania Germans had not helped him overcome a pronounced Rhenish Bavarian accent. Of it his biographer, a stickler for correctness, has commented amusingly: "With a stubbornness worthy of a better cause, he retained his original Palatine dialect, which gave his speech a pleasantly comical accent...If his English was fluent and yet entirely foreign sounding, his German was even more comical." One can readily appreciate how his contacts with the Rhineland, his acquaintances among the Pennsylvania Germans who in turn had roots there, plus his public position and willingness to aid his countrymen, made Dorsheimer the magnet he became for German immigrants in the 1830's. Thus started a movement that was to continue of its own momentum after his departure.

Along the canal to the west of Lyons, especially in Rochester and Buffalo, the Germans settled in even greater numbers. They are said to have accounted for almost a third the population of Rochester in the 1880's.[10] O. Turner, in his book of 1843 on The Holland Purchase, noted: "The location of German emigrants upon the Holland purchase, forms a prominent feature of recent events. In Buffalo, they already compose nearly one-third of the entire population and are mingled in almost all its branches of business..." (p. 662)

No wonder, then, that ambitious Philip Dorsheimer, assaying a larger sphere of action, removed to Buffalo in 1836. There he owned first the Farmers Hotel, then the Mansion House.[11] He acted as interpreter and negotiator for the Ebenezer Inspirationalists in their purchase of a large tract of land near Buffalo in 1842-3.[12] Riding on the rising tide of German immigrants and votes into the 1850's, the genial inn-keeper attained a wide political influence. A Buffalo account opines: "He knew how to convince the most respected Americans that he was the most influential German, not only in Buffalo but of the entire United States".[13] His biographer has given a first-hand observation on the picturesque part Dorsheimer played in the nomination of Fremont for President in 1856.

Having lived the good life in his adopted land, Philip Dorsheimer passed away in 1868, soon after the Civil War, at age 71. His one child, William born in Lyons in 1832, studied law and himself became prominent in New York politics, attaining to the Lieutenant-Governorship. Although the family name, Dorsheimer is not known to have survived from this line, it has from other branches in the U.S.A. Certainly there are many descendants of those immigrants whom Philip aided in Wayne County.

Among Those Who Came

Those who were influenced by Dorsheimer to come to Wayne County we cannot recall in numbers, but we can identify a few. One family is among the writer's ancestors, and it is this which has excited his interest and produced this little study: the family of John Espenschied (1781-1849) that arrived in 1835 and settled about a mile north of Alton, Sodus Township. The farm title was taken actually from Philip Dorsheimer and two associates, Cullen Foster and Daniel Chapman.[14] This, and the fact of the family having come from Siefersheim, a village adjacent to Dorsheimer's, is the indication of their having been attracted by him.

There is the further circumstances of the oldest son, John Espenscheid, Jr. having come the year before in the company of neighbors, the family of Conrad Young (1786-1862) that settled in Wayne Center. The passenger manifest of the ship on which the Youngs came in 1834 has been preserved.[15] Included in a long list of emigrees from Hesse-Darmstadt, is no less than Dorsheimer's father, "William Dorsheimer". The age given, 68, checks the Woellstein birth record (Evangelical Church). Here, then, is ample proof of the connection between the genial inn-keeper and these two families of Young (originally Jung) and Espenscheid (originally Espenschied).

The passenger list bears also the name "Jean Sauer" age 29. No country of origin is listed but apparently he was intended to be included among those from Hesse-Darmstadt. This person appears to have been John Sauer, one of three brothers reported to have come from near Bingen in 1834. They were John, Martin and Christopher Sauer, all of whom settled in Sodus Township, the latter subsequently removing westward.

A family that came also from Siefersheim, in 1836, is that of Henry Wagner (1793-1867). He and his wife Mary are buried in Ferguson's Corners. They are progenitors of Tusanelda Nusbickel, wife of Dr. Reuben Spencer Simpson of 65 Broad Street, Lyons. Her Nuesbickel immigrant ancestor, Frederick (1818-1897), emigrated in 1839 from Dorsheimer's native village of Woellstein, and lived in Sodus, Rose and Lyons.

Another family from the village Woellstein, arriving about 1837, is that of Rodenbach, Daniel (1808-1857) and wife Katharina Weppler, the parents of four children born "over there" and six more to be acquired here. His was an old flour-mill family, as had been Dorsheimer's and the ancestry has been traced far back in history. There were Rodenbachs that settled in Pennsylvania as there were Dorsheimers.[16]

Coming from a range of ten to fifteen miles

from Dorsheimer's home village, we find other migrants that may have been influenced by Dorsheimer: Dr. Franz L. Brunk was born in 1810 in Kanton Obermoschel in the Palatinate southwest of Woellstein. He migrated in 1834 to Lyons. There he married an American girl, removed to Indiana, thence to Buffalo where he practiced medicine and became a newspaper editor, and there he was introduced to Dorsheimer Gustav Koerner, to whom we are indebted for the inn-keeper's biography. Dr. Brunk finally returned to Germany, evidently disappointed in the "land of unlimited opportunity".[17]

Lastly, we recognize two more immigrants who may have owed their Lyons residence to Dorsheimer. John Hano, who in turn became an inn-keeper, stopped off from a canal boat upon seeing on the dock an old friend from his home town, Philip Althen. Althen is reported to have been born about 1810 in Gerbach, Rhine Bavaria, and to have migrated in 1835.[18] This village is some ten miles south of Dorsheimer's Wollenstein, on the brook Apfelbach, in the Rhine Palatinate. Here we appear to have two more recruits to credit to the magnetic circle of the personable inn-keeper. Doubtless there were many more, and still more attracted secondarily.

Those from Alsace

In the several histories of Wayne County and Lyons, one finds mention of about a hundred German family names; and for about half of them the principality from which they came is given.[19] Some 20 are from Alsace, a number comparable to those from the Hesse-Darmstadt-Palatinate region of Dorsheimer. Alsace is fully fifty miles south, up the Rhine, so it is not likely the Alsatians had been influenced by the example of Dorsheimer. How was it then, that they came to Wayne; was it "happenstance", or was there a chain from a forerunner?

Alsatians of German extraction were then leaving their native land for the same general reasons as their racial kin to the north - plus an additional spur: their country had been annexed by the French. The population of Alsace had been Teutonic from Roman times, but had been conquered by France under Louis XIV in his push to chastise the Protestants and advance his border to the Rhine, in the 1600's.[20] That the Alsatians of the 1800's were still Germanic we have evidence from a German intellectual who fled through norther Alsace from the Frankfurt uprising of 1833 - the aforementioned Koerner. He found that "In Weissenburg, as well as Lauterburg, everybody, even the government employees, spoke German. Indeed, there was no difference at all in language and manners between the Alsantians of that time and the people of Laudau or Neustadt" (of the Palatinate).[21] No wonder, then, that those coming to Wayne from Alsace, although born under the tri-colors, regarded themselves as Germanic and intermarried with the Germans.

We cannot answer the question of how the

Alsatians were directed to Wayne, nor do we know their numbers to have been any greater, proportionately, than in other areas of the USA. But we know of one family that is interesting as an example. George Henry Ramige was born in Hatten, near Strasburg, Alsace, 1788 January 6th. He married there in 1809 Maria Salome Kuntz. With seven children they migrated to Lyons in 1829. He and his wife were among the founders of the Lyons Evangelical Church in 1835, along with Michael and Rosina Faulstich, George and Dorothy Stoetzel, George and Catherine Humbert, George Ramige (son) and wife Barbara, and Philip Lang. Reflecting the more liberal element of the Calvinists of the Rhineland is the Lyon's report that "The Church met strong opposition for a continued period from German people to whom its tenants savored of revolution".

Removal West

This George H. Ramige, in 1848 at age 60, led a family group from Lyons to the Illinois Country where they formed a new colony, at Groveland near Peoria. (In 1883 his oldest son of like name in turn removed farther west with his family, to Rockwell City, Iowa - westward the course of Empire!) One of the daughters of George Sr. had married in Wayne County Karl Espencheid, a son of the John of Alton previously mentioned. Two daughters of George Sr. had married in Wayne respectively two Eller brother immigrants; and the youngest child of George Sr., Frederick, married in Groveland a sister of the Eller boys. These three

Ellers, John, Nicholas, and Anna Maria, had been born in Wonsheim, a village a mile or two south of Siefersheim, as is Woellstein north.[22] Here was intermarriage between some of Dorsheimer's countrymen and Alsatians, as well as removal westward.

Michigan had been a goal of migration since the 1830's as already indicated, and appears to have been also an objective of removal out of Wayne.[23] Of the Conrad Young family that arrived in 1834 - the oldest son Cassimer, came as an advance scout the year before, and then settled in Michigan, Jackson County, Concord Township, to be followed later by his brother John. Around 1890 when Alfred S. Roe was making his remarkable human inventory of Rose Township, he found many of the older Yankee settlement families removed westward. In mentioning a family that moved to Michigan he observed:

"The continuous migration westward of some families seems almost startling. Alaska offers new opportunities for those, who, till its purchase, had to stop in California."[24]

Something which continues to sound familiar to us today is related by the author, of a widow with a farm on her hands and a large family:

"She tells me, however, that the boys of today don't like the farm, and she cannot get hired help to do as she would like."[25]

To Emigrate or Not?

The question of emigrating naturally had been a momentous one in the first place for the Rhinelanders. Something of the care with which it was considered is revealed in an old Germanscript letter which has come down to the writer.[26] It is addressed to his maternal great-grandfather, the previously mentioned John Espencheid of Alton, who had migrated from Siefersheim in 1835. It bears the date of 1st March, 1840 and was written from the village adjoining Siefersheim on the south, Wonsheim. The writer was a brother of John's wife (then dead), Johannes Fitting, who evidently was considering pulling up stakes, but it is not known that he did so. He asks of his brother-in-law in Alton:

"I would like to have you conscientiously answer me if you think it would repay to go to all this trouble? Is there any prospect that one could buy sufficient farm land for the money obtained by selling our land here, which would produce something in value and quality? It is said here that Konrad Jung has lost his property. If this is the case please tell me about it." (This is the Conrad Young who had migrated in 1834; he may have had to surrender some of his property in the depression of 1837; not all was roseate in the new world!)

Added at the end of this letter in a different hand, is a note by another relative, an uncle of the three Eller children mentioned above, two of whom are mentioned in it, Johannes and Nicholaus:

"My son Johannes, and the sons of Brother-in-law Eller Johannes and Nicholaus, are thinking of coming to you in the coming years and to learn some craft from you. Eller's son Peter had learned the craft of leather and also wants to come to you. Do you think all of this would be good for our children? As to all this let us have your opinion on which we firmly depend.

Johannes Eller"

In the letter as a whole we see the anxious questioning of one who had gone before, by relatives who were weighing the move in respect to their children. The two Eller sons, Johannes and Nicholaus, did migrate to Wayne in the 1840's, married there and removed westward as previously mentioned. Their brother Peter immigrated in the 1850's and settled in New York City, becoming a brewer, with descendants in New Jersey.

These are examples of the threads across the Atlantic out of Europe that have woven some of the human fabric of Wayne. There's no end to tracing them, but the identifying of individual strands is rewarding for their contribution to our heritage.

Lloyd Espencheid
99 - 82nd Road
Kew Gardens 15, N.Y.

REFERENCES AND NOTES:

1. A good summary of the early history of western New York is given in the introduction to the book "History of Western New York", by Rev. James H. Hotchkin, pub. 1848, although the text is confined to Presbyterian Church history. The more complete histories are, of course, those of O. Turner: "Holland Purchase", pub. 1849 and "Phelps and Gorham Purchase", pub. 1851.

2. An insight into what the overrunning of the Rhineland by the French meant to the inhabitants thereof has been given recently by the retired pastor of one of the local churches, Rev. Friedrich Pabst of Siefersheim, Rheinhessen, in Espencheid Family Paper No. 8, of March 1958, pp. 6-8.

3. Life in a cultured family of the Rhineland following Napoleon's time, participation in the idealistic upheaval of 1833, flight through France and across the Atlantic, passage inland along the Erie Canal, followed by a constructive new life in the middle-west of Lincoln's time and beyond - all is beautifully portrayed in the "Memoirs of Gustav Koerner 1809-1896", 2 vols., pub. by Torch Press, Cedar Rapids, Iowa, 1909.

4. Faust, Albert B., "The German Element in the United States", 2 vols., 1909, Vol. 1, Chapter XVII, A Summary View.

5. Lieber, Francis: Letters to a Gentleman in Germany, Phila., 1834, p. 201.

6. Koerner, in reference 9 below, gives Dorsheimer's year of migration as 1816. But an obituary of his son William, says his father, Phillip, "came to this country from Germany in 1815, just before the battle of Waterloo, to escape the conscription of Napoleon." (N.Y. Tribune, 1888 March 28, clipping in Scrap Book of Franklin A. Jagger, Vol. 44, pp. 91-92, State Library, Albany, N.Y.)

7. "Geschichte der Deutschen in Buffalo...", pub. Rheinecke & Zesch, Buffalo, 1898, biographical part in German, p. 24; general part in English, p. 50.

8a. History of Wayne County, N.Y. pub. by Everts, Ensign & Everts, Phila., 1877, pp. 40, 100, 102.

8b. Landmarks of Wayne County, N.Y., edited by George W. Cowles, Syracuse, 1895, p. 239, pp. 239-241, with view showing Lyons Hotel as of 1840 on p. 242.

8c. Grips Historical Souvenier of Lyons, N.Y., 1904, pp. 39-40, 87, 102.

Additional pertinent Wayne County publications are: Wayne County Directory 1867-8, by Hamilton Child, pub. Syracuse, 1867 and The Rose Township Sketches of Reference 24 below.

9a. Koerner, Gustav: "Philipp Dorscheimer", in Der Deutsche Pioneer, Vol. 11, 1879, pp. 251-253.

9b. Koerner's "Das Deutsche Element...", 1880, pp. 140-143.

10. Peck, Wm. F.: "Semi-centennial History of Rochester...", Syracuse, 1884, Chapter XLVI by Herman Pfaefflin, p. 496.

11. "...the old Mansion House, rightly named...a spacious brick house, embowered in trees and shrubs and an old fashioned garden...from the windows and three story all-around piazzas of which the guests were wont to enjoy the view."

"The landlord was the portly, genial embodiment of a man, Philip Dorsheimer, then the most influential man among German citizens, and very popular with the best classes of Buffalonians."

(Mathews, Sylvester J.: "Memories of Early Days in Buffalo", Buffalo Hist. Soc. Pubs., Vol. 47, 1914, p. 198.)

12. Poltz, H.K., in The American-German Review, 1945, Aug., p. 18.

13. Reference 3, Vol 2, p. 16; also Reference 9.

14. Wayne County Clerk, Lyons, N.Y., Liber 18, Deeds, p. 230, dated 1835 Dec. 17.

15. Preserved in the National Archives, Washington, D.C.: Manifest of the Ship Normandie from Havre, arriving at the Port of New York 1834 August 22.

16. Ancestry of Miss Marion Klipple of 189 Canal St., Lyons, N.Y.

17. Reference 9-b, p. 144.

18. Reference 8-c, p. 102. Philip Althen is mentioned also in Reference 8-b, Part 1, p. 250.

19. Reference 8-b is rich in biographical sketches although with the many errors that do creep in.

20. Encyclopedia Britannica, 11th edition, 1910-11, Vol., p. 755.

21. Reference 3, Vol. 1, p. 242.

22. From a family tree chart of the "Eller Family & Relations...", accompanying a memorandum of 4 Jan. 1954 entitled:

"Groveland, Tazwell County, Ill., Its Settlement Out of Lyons, Wayne County, N.Y." Copy in N.Y. State Library, Albany; and in Wayne County Historical Archives, Lyons, N.Y.

23. Reference 8-c, Part 1, p. 249.

24. Roe, Alfred S.: "Rose Neighborhood Sketches", 1893, p. 224.

25. Reference 24, p. 218.

26. Photo-copy of German letter of 1840, translation and explanatory memo of 25 Nov. 1949 by the present writer, is deposited in State Library, Albany, and in Wayne County Hist. Archives, Lyons.

A letter published in the November 27th edition of the newspaper - following the first installment is quoted as follows:

THE NAME IS ROE

[To the] Editor: Lyons Republican and Clyde Times:

In the story on Early Wayne County Settlers by Mr. Lloyd Espenschied, in your issue of Nov. 20, he quotes from "Rose Neighborhood Sketches" by Alfred S. Rose. I would appreciate your correcting that name to Alfred Roe who was my mother's brother, she being the reason my middle name is Roe. Thank you.

s/Edmund Roe Johnson

www.ingramcontent.com/pod-product-compliance
Lightning Source LLC
Chambersburg PA
CBHW070756050426
42449CB00010B/2493